A Picture Book of Davy Crockett

David A. Adler

illustrated by John & Alexandra Wallner

SCHOLASTIC INC.
New York Toronto London Auckland Sydney
Mexico City New Delhi Hong Kong

Other books in David A. Adler's *Picture Book Biography* series

A Picture Book of George Washington
A Picture Book of Abraham Lincoln
A Picture Book of Martin Luther King, Jr.
A Picture Book of Benjamin Franklin
A Picture Book of Helen Keller
A Picture Book of Eleanor Roosevelt
A Picture Book of Christopher Columbus
A Picture Book of Florence Nightingale
A Picture Book of Jesse Owens
A Picture Book of Anne Frank
A Picture Book of Frederick Douglass
A Picture Book of Rosa Parks
A Picture Book of Sojourner Truth
A Picture Book of John F. Kennedy
A Picture Book of Simón Bolívar
A Picture Book of Harriet Tubman

To Pam Conrad, who makes words dance
D. A. A.

To our friend John Green
J. W. & A. W.

ISBN 0-439-27623-3

 Published by Scholastic Inc., 555 Broadway, New York, NY 10012, by arrangement with Holiday House, Inc. SCHOLASTIC and associated logos are trademarks and/or registered trademarks of Scholastic Inc.

12 11 10 9 8 7 6 5 4 3 2 1 2 3 4 5 6/0

Printed in the U.S.A. 08

First Scholastic printing, January 2001

According to the legends told about Davy Crockett, he leaped out of his cradle the day he was born and said, "I'm Davy Crockett, fresh from the backwoods. I'm half horse, half alligator, with a little touch of snapping turtle. I can ride a streak of lightning and whip my weight in wildcats. I can outfight, outshoot, outjump any man in the country. And I will!"

This fantastic tale and many others were based on the life of a real Davy Crockett who was a great storyteller. His habit of telling tall tales about himself led to the legends.

The real Davy Crockett was born on August 17, 1786, in a backwoods cabin in eastern Tennessee. His parents were John and Rebecca Crockett, poor farmers. David's father had been a soldier in the Revolutionary War. David was the fifth of their nine children.

When David was about seven, his family moved to the mouth of Cove Creek. There his father and a partner built a mill. But just as it was being finished, a flood destroyed it.

The family moved again, to Jefferson County, Tennessee. There, along the road from Abingdon to Knoxville, John Crockett opened a tavern, a place for people traveling by to stop, eat, and rest.

In 1798 a Dutchman stopped at the Crockett tavern. He was traveling to Virginia with all his belongings, including a herd of cattle. He needed help.

John Crockett hired David out to the Dutchman. David was twelve years old. He had not been away from his home and family before. He wrote later that he "set out with a heavy heart."

When David returned home many weeks later, he was a changed boy. The Dutchman had taught him to handle and shoot a long rifle. David would become a great hunter and one of the best shots in the country.

The next fall David's parents sent him to a small school that had opened near the Crockett tavern. He didn't stay long. On his fourth day there, Davy got into a fight. He was sure the teacher would whip him for fighting, so he skipped school. When David's father found out he wasn't going to school, he went after David with a stick. David ran away.

David was gone for almost two years. He did farmwork, drove cattle, helped out on a wagon train, and worked for a hatter.

When David returned home, he sat at the tavern dinner table with the paying guests. At first, no one recognized him. But then his sister cried out, "Here is my lost brother," and gave him a big welcome-home hug.

David's father made good use of his son's return. He hired David out to work for Abraham Wilson and John Kennedy. David's work paid off debts his father owed these men.

David didn't like working at Wilson's place. But he liked working for Kennedy. After his father's debt was paid, David went back to work for Kennedy. With the money he earned, he bought clothes, a horse, and a rifle.

John Kennedy's son had a small school. There David finally learned to read, write, and do simple arithmetic.

David often entered shooting matches and usually won. He was at a party after one shooting match when, in his words, "an old Irish woman . . . came up to me and began to praise my red cheeks and said she had a sweetheart for me." The sweetheart was Mary ("Polly") Finley, the Irishwoman's daughter. David soon fell in love with Polly.

On August 12, 1806, just before his twentieth birthday, David and Polly were married. They had three children, John Wesley, William, and Margaret.

David and Polly lived in a log cabin near Elk River, Tennessee. Polly worked a spinning wheel. David tended a small farm and he hunted. David loved to hunt, especially bear. He called his gun "Old Betsy," and with it he killed enough wild animals to feed his family and his neighbors.

In 1813 the Creeks, a tribe of Native Americans, upset at losing their land to white settlers, attacked Fort Mims in Alabama. Hundreds of settlers were killed.

There was a call for men to fight the Creeks. David volunteered. He was a soldier and scout under the command of General Andrew Jackson. David hunted, too, and provided the soldiers with plenty of meat. He also entertained the men at night with stories.

The Creek War ended in 1814 with the defeat of the Native Americans at the Battle of Horseshoe Bend.

David returned home and worked on his farm. Then, in 1815, his wife Polly became ill. David wrote later that this was his "hardest trial . . . death entered my humble cottage and tore from my children an affectionate good mother, and from me a tender and loving wife."

When Polly died, her youngest child, Margaret, was just a baby. David decided he needed a wife to help raise Margaret and his other children.

A widow with two young children lived nearby. Her husband had been killed in battle. Her name was Elizabeth Patton.

David described Elizabeth as a "good industrious woman." David courted her and in 1816 they married. David and Elizabeth had three children together, Robert, Rebecca, and Matilda.

In 1817 David, Elizabeth, and their children moved west to the head of Shoal Creek in Lawrence County, Tennessee. This was frontier land with many new settlers. There was no law, so settlers set up a temporary government. David was appointed judge.

David Crockett never studied law, but he was a success as a judge. He based his decisions on common sense and honesty.

David was popular. In 1821 he was asked to run for a seat in the state legislature.

Politics was "bran-fire new business," to David Crockett. He wrote, "I had never read even a newspaper in my life, or anything else on the subject. But over all my difficulties, it seems to me, I was born for luck." He won the seat.

In 1822 David Crockett moved with his family even farther west to the shore of the Obion River. It was good hunting land.

In 1827 David Crockett had more "luck" with politics. He was elected to the United States House of Representatives. He was reelected in 1829 and 1833.

Davy Crockett went to Washington. There he often wore his frontier clothes, his leather pants and coonskin cap.

Andrew Jackson, David's commanding officer in the Creek War, was president. President Jackson was pushing hard to get a bill passed that would take land away from Native Americans. It was land promised to them earlier, when they signed a peace treaty. David called Jackson's bill a "wicked, unjust measure." He voted against it. He opposed the president on other measures, too, and became a political enemy of the Jackson Democrats.

The Whig party thought David Crockett would be a good candidate for president. Many people felt David's favorite motto, "Be sure you're right, then go ahead," reflected the spirit of the nation. David Crockett toured several eastern cities, looking for more supporters. But the Jackson forces worked against him. He was defeated in the congressional election of 1835. David wrote, "I never saw such means used to defeat any candidate, as were put in practice against me . . . I was completely rascalled out of my election."

David Crockett was angry. He was through with politics and ready for new adventure. He announced, "As my country no longer requires my services, I have made up my mind to go to Texas."

In 1835 Texas was not part of his country, the United States. It belonged to Mexico.

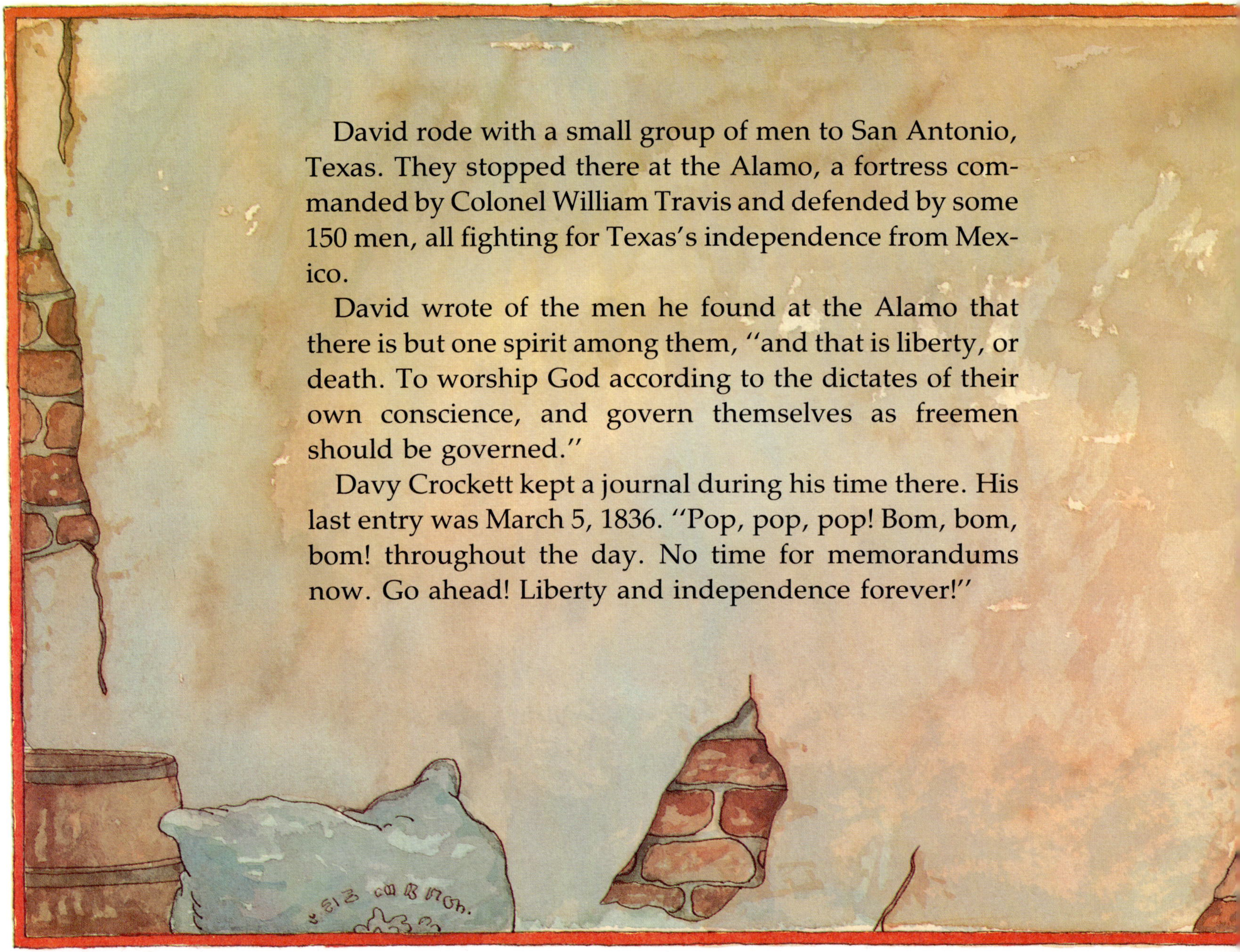

David rode with a small group of men to San Antonio, Texas. They stopped there at the Alamo, a fortress commanded by Colonel William Travis and defended by some 150 men, all fighting for Texas's independence from Mexico.

David wrote of the men he found at the Alamo that there is but one spirit among them, "and that is liberty, or death. To worship God according to the dictates of their own conscience, and govern themselves as freemen should be governed."

Davy Crockett kept a journal during his time there. His last entry was March 5, 1836. "Pop, pop, pop! Bom, bom, bom! throughout the day. No time for memorandums now. Go ahead! Liberty and independence forever!"

The next day more than five thousand Mexican soldiers attacked the Alamo. According to one report, all the defenders of the fortress, including Davy Crockett, were killed in battle. According to another report, when the battle ended, six men fighting for the independence of Texas, including David Crockett, survived. Soon after he was taken prisoner, David Crockett was attacked by one dozen enemy soldiers who stabbed and killed him with their swords.

After David Crockett died, his legend grew. For more than twenty years *Davy Crockett Almanacs* were published. Each almanac had useful information followed by tall tales.

According to the tales told about him, Davy Crockett was born weighing more than two hundred pounds. He had a pet bear named Death Hug and a pet buffalo named Mississip. Davy rode a sea serpent from Cape Cod to Washington, and taught a cougar, an alligator, a wolf, and some rabbits to dance. The legendary Davy Crockett was a great frontiersman. The real David Crockett was a great frontiersman, too.

AUTHOR'S NOTE

Many of the quotes from David Crockett reprinted here were taken from his autobiography, *Narrative of the Life of David Crockett,* first published in 1834.

David Crockett was invited to visit Harvard University, but he would not go there. He feared they would give him an honorary degree. "I had never taken any degree, and did not own to any except a small degree of good sense not to pass for what I was not—I would not go for it."

At the Alamo, Davy Crockett met Colonel Jim Bowie "whose name," Crockett wrote, "has been given to a knife." Crockett wrote of the bowie knife, "I wish I may be shot if the bare sight of it wasn't enough to give a man of a squeamish stomach the colic, especially before breakfast." Bowie was one of the men killed at the Alamo.

David Crockett's eldest son, John Wesley Crockett (1807–1852), followed his father into Congress. He represented western Tennessee for two terms, 1837–1841.

IMPORTANT DATES

1786	Born in eastern Tennessee on August 17.
1806	Married Polly Finley.
1815	Wife Polly died.
1816	Married Elizabeth Patton.
1821–1824	Served in the Tennessee state legislature.
1827	First elected to the United States Congress. He was reelected in 1829 and 1833.
1834	Tours New York City, Boston, and Philadelphia.
1836	Killed at the Alamo, San Antonio, Texas, on March 6.
1835 or 1836	The *Crockett Almanacs* first appear.